How and do animals eat?

Bobbie Kalman

Crabtree Publishing Company

www.crabtreebooks.com

All About Animals Close-Up

Dedicated by Bobbie and Peter
For Hailey Joy Sikkens,
who has brought her parents much joy,
but we miss her Mommy, Crystal, a lot!

Author and editor-in-chief
Bobbie Kalman

Publishing plan research and development
Reagan Miller

Editor
Kathy Middleton

Proofreader
Crystal Sikkens

Design
Bobbie Kalman
Katherine Berti
Samantha Crabtree (cover)

Photo research
Bobbie Kalman

Print and production coordinator
Katherine Berti

Photographs
Digital Vision: page 20
Dreamstime: page 9
iStockphoto: page 17 (top)
All other images by Shutterstock

Library and Archives Canada Cataloguing in Publication

Kalman, Bobbie, author
    How and what do animals eat? / Bobbie Kalman.

(All about animals close-up)
Includes index.
Issued in print and electronic formats.
ISBN 978-0-7787-0543-7 (bound).--ISBN 978-0-7787-0597-0 (pbk.).--
ISBN 978-1-4271-7591-5 (pdf).--ISBN 978-1-4271-7586-1 (html)

    1. Animals--Food--Juvenile literature. I. Title.

QL756.5.K3428 2014   j591.5'3   C2014-903905-0
                                              C2014-903906-9

Library of Congress Cataloging-in-Publication Data

Kalman, Bobbie.
  How and what do animals eat? / Bobbie Kalman.
     pages cm -- (All about animals close-up)
  Includes index.
  ISBN 978-0-7787-0543-7 (reinforced library binding) -- ISBN 978-0-7787-0597-0
(pbk.) -- ISBN 978-1-4271-7591-5 (electronic pdf) -- ISBN 978-1-4271-7586-1
(electronic html)
  1. Animals--Food--Juvenile literature. I. Title.

QL756.5.K348 2014
590--dc23
                                              2014022878

Crabtree Publishing Company

Printed in the U.S.A./092014/JA20140811

www.crabtreebooks.com   1-800-387-7650

Published in Canada
Crabtree Publishing
616 Welland Ave.
St. Catharines, Ontario
L2M 5V6

Published in the United States
Crabtree Publishing
PMB 59051
350 Fifth Avenue, 59th Floor
New York, New York 10118

Published in the United Kingdom
Crabtree Publishing
Maritime House
Basin Road North, Hove
BN41 1WR

Published in Australia
Crabtree Publishing
3 Charles Street
Coburg North
VIC 3058

Contents

Why do animals eat?

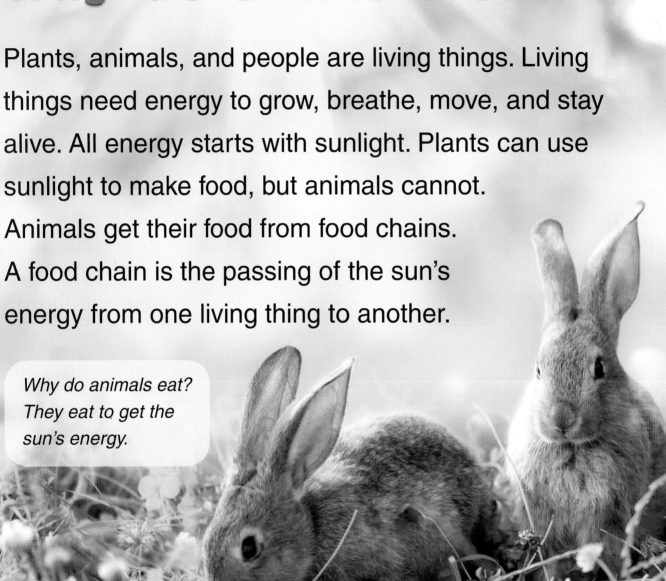

Plants, animals, and people are living things. Living things need energy to grow, breathe, move, and stay alive. All energy starts with sunlight. Plants can use sunlight to make food, but animals cannot.

Animals get their food from food chains.

A food chain is the passing of the sun's energy from one living thing to another.

Why do animals eat? They eat to get the sun's energy.

A food chain

sunlight

energy

Plants use the sun's energy to make food.

energy

The sun's energy is passed along to the rabbit when it eats the plants.

When the fox eats the rabbit, the sun's energy that was in the plants flows from the rabbit to the fox.

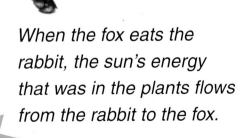

energy

What do animals eat?

Animals eat different kinds of foods. Some eat mainly plants. Plant-eaters are called **herbivores**. Some animals eat mainly other animals. Meat-eaters are called **carnivores**.

Squirrels eat mainly plant foods, such as fruit, nuts, and seeds.

Eating all kinds of food

Omnivores eat both plants and other animals, so these animals are able to find food more easily than herbivores or carnivores. This fox has hunted a squirrel to eat, but it also eats plants.

Food for babies

Many baby animals have to find their own food. Baby birds, however, are fed by their parents until they grow feathers and learn to fly. The babies then find their own food.

Mammal mothers, like this wolf mother, **nurse**, or feed their newborn babies milk from their bodies.

Grasses and leaves

Many herbivores eat grasses. Feeding on grasses is called **grazing**. Horses, sheep, and cows graze on grass. What do newborn foals, or baby horses, eat?

Horses are mammals. How do mammal mothers feed their babies?

An elephant uses its trunk to grab leaves.

Koalas spend most of their time in eucalyptus trees. There are over 800 kinds of eucalyptus trees, but koalas eat from only about 50 different kinds.

What are browsers?

Some herbivores eat leaves. Eating the leaves on bushes and trees is called **browsing**. Giraffes, elephants, and koalas are browsers.

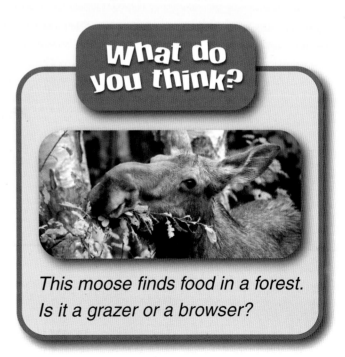

What do you think?

This moose finds food in a forest. Is it a grazer or a browser?

Nuts, fruit, and flowers

Squirrels and chipmunks have strong front teeth for cracking nuts and seeds.

Many herbivores and omnivores eat fruit, nuts, and seeds, as well as flowers. Some insects and birds drink **nectar**, a sweet liquid found inside flowers.

Chipmunks carry their food home in their huge cheeks.

This field mouse is eating fruit. The mouse holds the small berry in its paws.

Rabbits are herbivores that eat leaves, green plants, and flowers.

Hummingbird moths drink nectar through their long **proboscis**, which is like a straw.

What do you think?

Which animals eat food the way you do? How and where do you store your food?

13

Predators hunt prey

Predators are carnivores or omnivores that hunt other animals to eat. The animals they hunt are called **prey**. Predators can be large animals, such as alligators, or small animals, such as lizards. Some predators eat mainly insects (see pages 16–17).

Alligators spend a lot of time in water, where they hunt fish to eat. Their sharp teeth can also chew large prey.

cheetahs

antelope

The cheetahs on the right are hunting an antelope. They are fast runners that can chase fast prey.

What do you think?

Are herbivores predators or prey? Why do you think so? Name four predators and five prey.

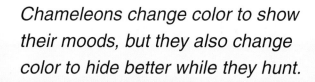

Chameleons change color to show their moods, but they also change color to hide better while they hunt.

A mole eats mainly earthworms and other small animals that live in the soil. To find prey, a mole uses its sharp claws to dig through dirt.

Catching insects

Insect-eaters catch insects in different ways. Some birds catch insects while they are flying. Some predators, such as spiders and lizards, catch insects that visit plants for food. Other predators dig up insects that live under the ground, such as grubs.

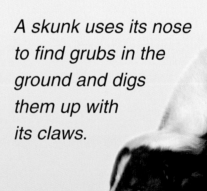

A skunk uses its nose to find grubs in the ground and digs them up with its claws.

A jumping spider jumps up to catch a fly with its legs.

grub   *claws*

This small lizard hunts insects that visit flowers to look for food.

This frog catches flies and other insects with its long, sticky tongue.

What do you think?

Name the animals that catch insects by:
- smelling and digging
- jumping
- using a sticky tongue
- hiding on plants

Different body parts

Different body parts help animals get and eat their food. Some animals, like this monkey, have teeth for chewing. Eagles and hawks have excellent eyesight that allows them to see their prey from the sky.

This eagle spotted a fish from high above the water. It swooped down and grabbed its prey using its talons, or sharp claws.

Bird beaks

Birds use their beaks to catch, scoop, or drink their food. Their beaks suit the foods they eat.

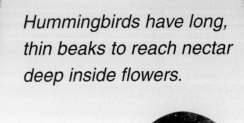

Hummingbirds have long, thin beaks to reach nectar deep inside flowers.

These birds used their sharp beaks to catch a spider and a crab.

throat pouch

A pelican has a long beak and large throat pouch that it uses for catching fish. The water drains through the pouch, and the bird then swallows its prey.

Using tools

Animals use their body parts to help them eat food, but some animals also use tools. Rocks and sticks are two tools that animals use to get the food they need. Apes, such as the chimpanzee below, use sticks to pull termites and ants from their mounds, or dirt homes.

Sea otters use rocks to break open the shells of the clams they eat. They carry the rocks on their bodies.

Leopards use trees as a place to eat and store their food away from other animals.

These monkeys are using the stones on this beach to crack open sea snails.

How do we eat?

Which animals find fruit to eat in trees?

Which animals in this book find food or eat it the way these children are doing?

Which animal stuffs food in its cheeks the way this boy is doing?

Which animal uses sticks for picking up and eating its food?

Which animals drink through body parts that look like straws?

Learning more

Books

Kalman, Bobbie. *Baby Carnivores* (It's fun to learn about baby animals). Crabtree Publishing Company, 2013.

Kalman, Bobbie. *Rapping about what animals eat* (Rapping about...). Crabtree Publishing Company, 2012.

Kalman, Bobbie. *How do living things find food?* (Introducing Living Things). Crabtree Publishing Company, 2011.

Kalman, Bobbie. *What is a Herbivore?* (Big Science Ideas). Crabtree Publishing Company, 2008.

Kalman, Bobbie. *What is an Omnivore?* (Big Science Ideas). Crabtree Publishing Company, 2008.

Bozzo, Linda. *Amazing Animal Teeth* (Creature Features). PowerKids Press, 2008.

Llewellyn, Claire. *Food Webs: Who Eats Who?* (Show Me Science), Raintree Perspectives, 2014.

Websites

NatureWorks: The Wildlife Web II - Herbivores and Carnivores
www.nhptv.org/natureworks/nwep10.htm

LiveScience: 10 Animals That Use Tools
www.livescience.com/9761-10-animals-tools.html

Ducksters: Ecosystem: Food Chain and Food Web
www.ducksters.com/science/ecosystems/food_chain_and_web.php

Words to know

browsing (BROU-zing) verb Feeding on the leaves of bushes and trees

carnivore (KAHR-nuh-vawr) noun An animal that eats mainly meat

grazing (GREY-zing) verb Feeding on grasses

herbivore (HUR-buh-vawr) noun An animal that eats mainly plants

nectar (NEK-ter) noun A sweet liquid found in flowers

nurse (nurs) verb To feed a newborn baby milk from the body; to drink milk from one's mother's body

omnivore (OM-nuh-vawr) noun An animal that eats both plants and other animals

predator (PRED-uh-tawr) noun An animal that hunts other animals for food

prey (prey) noun An animal that is hunted by another animal

proboscis (proh-BOS-kis) noun The long mouth part on some insects that is used for sucking

A noun is a person, place, or thing. A verb is an action word that tells you what someone or something does.

Index